DEDICATION

I am happy to say that there are too many to list as influencers to me and of this book. However, there are three I must acknowledge, first to my friend of over fifty years, Grady Bryant. We met in college, facing numerous challenges from our parents, friends, classmates, and everything involved in a relationship. To Benjamin Hicks, who allowed me to call him my son, and for him to call me his father. And lastly, my wife Diane, who stood by me for over forty-nine years. When I became frustrated by those who wished I would fail in the writing of this book, her unselfish love urged me on. As I've told others many times, a crown awaits her arrival at her heavenly home—but it is not a typical crown—a large, magnificent one that requires two or more people to hold upon her head. I will be forever grateful!

TABLE OF CONTENTS

Introduction:

I wish to share the acts of a wonderful, faithful, and forgiving God. One who *"is not like men...*[1]*"* A God who loves his children despite their many shortcomings. As a child of God, I have had many deliberate moments of unfaithfulness and deceitfulness towards Him and others. Despite these moments, I continue to experience His everlasting love and forgiveness. As you read, you will witness how this wonderful, faithful, and forgiving God taught my family and me to trust Him in all things and, most importantly, to be good stewards of the money entrusted to us.

People from all walks of life, including those of different races, social standings, and political influences, as well as those with good jobs and money in the bank, would do well to consider how they approach the use of their money carefully, especially in this social and financial climate, where one's use of money is closely examined. How an individual handles money serves as a blueprint for many to assess the reliability and trustworthiness of that

---

[1] Numbers 23:19

individual. One way many use to measure an individual's trustworthiness is the "Credit Score." In the last twenty years, credit scores have become the dominating force determining an individual's standing within the financial world. To obtain and maintain the necessities of life, it is essential to have a good credit score. Forbes Advisors, one of the top five financial advisors for 2023, states that credit scores range between 350 and 850. [2] However, a good credit score is over 700.[3]

Good credit works well for lenders, service providers, and the individual. For lenders and service providers, it assures that the individual will maintain excellent financial health throughout the term of the financial agreement. It gives them the peace of mind of a solid financial return. For the individual, it helps them avoid high-security deposits while securing low-interest rates and low down payments, along with the goodwill of the provider and service provider.[4] Having a poor credit score affects multiple financial aspects. First, it will influence lenders and service providers to charge higher

[2] What Is A Bad Credit Score? – Forbes Advisor
[3] Ibid
[4] Ibid

interest rates when one applies for mortgages and car loans. In addition, it can hinder an individual from renting an apartment, obtaining employment, or even obtaining an account with a utility company.

Many people find ways to secure stability due to the need for financial peace. Some will see it through hard work and a never-give-up attitude. They will sacrifice their present needs and desires by paying off debts and controlling unnecessary spending. Others will fall prey to financial exploiters who substitute financial stability with economic prosperity. These exploiters aim to con many through financial schemes. Some of the most successful include the Nigerian Letter or 419 scams, Ponzi schemes, Pyramid schemes, and Telemarketing fraud. Exploiters can even be found in churches. Church members trust their Church leaders, unthinkingly sacrificing their hard-earned money in hopes of achieving financial stability. Sadly, many do not achieve financial stability because their funds are diverted directly into the pockets of these exploiters. This book is not written to pursue economic prosperity, but to achieve financial stability through financial peace.

I write not as a financial adviser. Nor have I taken accounting courses or worked in a financial institution. What I possess are two essential ideas. First is the power of faith that God supplies to manage my family's finances boldly. **Faith,** stated in **Hebrews 11:6,** *But without faith, it is impossible to please Him: for He that cometh to God must believe that He is and that He is a rewarder of them that diligently seek Him.*[5] The text explains that faith begins with the conviction that God is real, living, and active in the world, without wavering or doubting. And He rewards those who conscientiously seek after him. The verse is one of the many I call "Personal Life Verses."[6] This verse, in 1975, first motivated me to propose to my wife, Diane. Then, the verse in 1989 swayed me to my lack of financial structure and health, which encouraged me to trust God to correct them. Second, I have experience managing family finances during success and failure. In **Philippians 4:11-13,** it states, *"Not that I speak in respect of want: for I have learned, in whatsoever state I am, in addition to that to be contented. I know both how to be abased, and I know how to abound: everywhere and in all things, I am instructed both to be full*

---

[5] King James Bible Translation
[6] A life verse, a personal biblical verse or verses giving encouragement directing an individual through life.

and to be hungry, both to abound and to suffer need. I can do all things through Christ, which strengthened me." [7] This timely truth, credited to the Apostle Paul, says Christ gives strength to overcome all of life's issues. There are the fruits and challenges of life. The fruits of life are the success stories we hear when someone wins the lottery or feels the blessings of the Lord. The challenges of life can be when one faces the loss of home, family, and friends. God is there for both, but He seems more involved with the challenges where He continues to give strength. Especially when an unsteady financial world tests hope, courage, and faith. Though pressed with many personal, family, and economic challenges, I stood firm in handling the challenges in the strength of the Lord. Experiencing both the challenges and the fruits of life made me a stronger person and a living witness to the power and grace of God.

Again, I have no formal training in financial planning. I pray that the lessons learned from this book, through my faith in God and personal experiences, will help you, the reader, develop a financial plan. It's not just a plan that uses gimmicks or get-rich schemes. I will not ask you to "name and claim it" or "sow seeds." Instead, it is a

---

[7] King James Translation

program that provides you with tools to achieve financial peace by placing money in the bank, providing for your family, developing plans for relaxation and enjoyment, and escaping the embarrassment of bankruptcy and colossal debt, or, as earlier stated, **financial peace**. Though written for Christians, it can help anyone seeking a plan to overcome economic encounters.

I give all praise and glory to God, who does everything well. Amen!

PART ONE:

TESTIMONIAL

Revelation 12:11, And they overcame him because of the blood of the Lamb and because of the word of their testimony, and they did not love their life *even* when faced with death. New American Standard Bible

Chapter One:

Proving a Need!

I need help

Psalm 107:28-30, *"Then they cry unto the Lord in their trouble, and he bringeth them out of their distresses. He maketh the storm a calm so that the waves thereof are still. Then are they glad because they are quiet; so, he bringeth them unto their desired haven."- King James Version!*

My wife Diane and I became aware of our financial
peace needs following our son's adoption. After ten years
of marriage without children, on December 15, 1986, we
brought this eleven-month-old male child into our home.
We named him Benjamin, after a biblical character who
exercises godliness and faith. We were both employed.
Diane, a full-time employee, and I worked part-time at a
Christian elementary school. Additionally, I studied part-
time at the Geneva College Center for Urban Theological
Studies (CUTS) in Philadelphia, Pennsylvania. Encouraged
and assisted by the adoption agency, I placed my education
on hold, securing full-time employment. The two full-time
employment incomes help cover the added expense of the
adoption and its aftermath, allowing us to avoid living
paycheck to paycheck. They also strengthen our interest-
bearing checking account, enabling us to pay bills on time
and plan affordable vacations. However, it did not provide
answers regarding our future. Diane and I defined
spending as "thinking in the moment." Now, with a child in
our lives, we recognize the need to plan. We need a
financial configuration that includes secure monetary
accounts for short- and long-term savings, enjoyable
vacations, the family's education, retirement, and a house.
However, Diane and I quickly realized that the house

would become the initial need. Living in a one-bedroom apartment, our son would soon need a bedroom and a backyard to play in. Also, a house would be the foundation that proves our seriousness regarding financial peace. It would serve as collateral as we explore other economic opportunities. We immediately prayed to the Lord for directions. In April of 1987, we examined a potential house.

The house was in the southeastern section of the city. There, the town was fulfilling promises of urban improvements. Old homes and factory buildings were either demolished or rehabbed, making way for single and multi-family housing, business/professional office spaces, and shopping areas, with street, water, and sewer improvements. The house in question borders the urban improvements and needs repairs. As my family and I inspected the house, we found the first-floor living room area leaning to one side of the room; the cause was the need for floor joint replacement. The second-floor bathroom had a hole, twelve inches wide, in the ceiling, allowing one to see the sky. Lastly, the home needed a new heating system. The asking price was five thousand dollars, with the seller asking for a one-thousand-dollar down payment and monthly payments of two hundred dollars until the debt was paid. Being young and inexperienced, unaware of how I would come up with the money, and in a hurry to obtain it, I seriously considered the house. Praise the Lord, a terrible mistake was prevented. Upon investigation, the house's seller was not the owner; the legal owner had died three months prior. The seller, an unscrupulous relative, took it upon herself to benefit from a relative's death. In addition, the house was in probate with numerous liens.[8] Though disappointed, Diane and I continued to look and pray. Three weeks later, another house was brought to our attention.

A missionary pastor friend referred us to his female relative, who had a house for rent in a working-class family neighborhood in the city's western section. The owner, who was moving to Binghamton, New York, with three small children, needed money to maintain a living income. After contacting her, we learned of her willingness to sell the house, as is, if we lease for one year. Diane and I became excited. Though the house needed cosmetic and maintenance improvements, we agreed. A one-year lease

---

[8] Legal declaration placed on a property belonging to the person who owns a debt. Said property cannot be sold or transferred to another until the debt is discharged.

was signed with the option to own. We moved in on June 1, 1987, with help from friends and family. November 15, 1987, Benjamin's adoption became legal. The excitement of adopting Benjamin and entering a house we could eventually own clouded our minds about the later problems of the neighborhood's depravity and the debt upon our home.

Gun violence, prostitution, and drugs controlled the neighborhood. A man was shot across the street from the family's house, with the perpetrator escaping along the alley behind the backyard of our home. Prostitutes and Drug dealers walked the community, soliciting customers, operating visually from the family's living room window. In the spring of 1988, advocating for social change, I joined a neighborhood watch group. Though prostitution was a menace to the community, drugs were seen as the main threat. On Friday evenings, when the weather was favorable, the group would assemble on the corner a block from my family's home to discourage illegal drug sales. The initial group included men who lived in the neighborhood. Including myself, a prison correction officer, a retiree, and two self-made businessmen. The group's consistency soon caught the eye of a drug gang. In

August of 1988, during a planned Friday evening "take back the neighborhood night," a gang member walked up to the group, threatening by saying, **"My gun is bigger than yours."** Sensing trouble, the group rushed to their homes, arming themselves with pistols and long guns. Two of the men's wives from the watch group were sensible and called the police. Soon afterward, four police vehicles sped down the street, chasing two cars carrying drug gang members with a cache of weapons. The wives' quick action prevented deaths. Subsequently, the neighborhood group grew with additional people from the neighborhood. However, the most notable addition was a police officer who taught self-defense training. He provided an uncrewed patrol car in plain sight whenever the group met. I stayed with the group for another year, but the sales of drugs continued. Though the gangs, drug sales, prostitution, and crime violence were enough to discourage living in the neighborhood, I was reminded of a story I heard from a missionary ministering in a gang-controlled public housing complex. The missionary wanted to impact the lives of people who needed the saving power of Jesus Christ but were living in poverty and crime. The missionary stated it did not make sense to go into the housing complex every morning to minister the saving power of Christ and leave every evening to the comfort of wealth and surplus of his suburban home. The missionary moved his family into the housing project. I don't know what happened to the missionary or his family. So, I don't know if he continued to live there or minister. I thought the Lord wanted me to do likewise, so staying seemed to be the spiritual option. It took an unseen, unplanned event to convince me that living in the neighborhood was not an option.

It began three months into the lease. The landlord instructed the tenant to send the monthly rent payment to an address in another state. For the next eight months, additional requests were sent by the landlord from five different addresses located in four states. Though concerned with the landlord's constant moves, Diane and I were more concerned with buying the house. As we entered the end of the first year, we discovered that the house had numerous welfare liens from each of the four states. As mentioned earlier, the liens made securing a clear, clean title impossible, thus making the house unsellable. We negotiated with the landlord to stay in the house for six months, paying rent and hoping to find a new home. But Praise the Lord! On the month the agreement ended, my family received an early surprise Christmas gift. Our landlord, showing compassion, gave her blessings by allowing us to live in the house **rent-free** until we purchased a new home. We would continue to be responsible for paying the monthly electric and gas bills. We discovered that we could be exempt from paying the water bill because it was in the landlord's name. The water could not be turned off for non-payment if it was documented that a special needs child was living in the home. Eight months into the adoption, Benjamin was diagnosed with Sickle Cell Disease. The money saved from not having a water bill gave us additional savings. However, we were financially responsible for all home maintenance and repairs.

1989 brought a telephone call to the late radio personality Herb Denenberg, proving to be the salvation of the family's housing pursuit. Mr. Denenberg was a consumer advocate and public affairs reporter for Radio and Television Stations WCAU, Philadelphia, PA.[9]. During one of his weekend radio call-in shows, I called Mr. Denenberg and asked how to purchase an affordable home. His answer opened my eyes to my ignorance of the housing market. He asked, ***"How much money do you have to***

---

[9] https://en.wikipedia.org/wiki/Herb_Denenberg, 1/31/2019

make a down payment for a house?" Thinking momentarily, I replied, *"Maybe one hundred dollars."* Truthfully but bluntly, he explained that a hundred dollars is insufficient to purchase "a shack." However, he showed sympathy for my situation by asking questions about my family's income, expenses, and spending habits. I shared that Diane and I were both gainfully employed, had no vast debts, and were free from paying rent or mortgage. In addition, we lacked a spending structure and a savings plan. Upon receiving our answers, he advised the following for the next eighteen months:

- Save two weeks of take-home pay from one of the two paychecks and deposit the money into a separate" no-touch "savings account. I later called this account "New Home."
- Review spending habits. Ask, "Is the family spending on things they need or want?"
- Develop a plan to track spending by writing it down on paper and religiously following it.

If consistently practiced, the family should have a sufficient down payment for a new home.

For eighteen months, Diane and I worked hard to save. The first two months were tough. Money in the "New Home" savings account eliminated the self-interest impulse to spend. And, it causes the family to review and then rethink spending. We learn to live within our means. We did not pay less, but we made wise choices. We stop impulse spending. We shop in thrift stores and compare prices. We began to understand the question, "Do we need this?" Seeing money left over and feeling secure, we decided on two radical actions six months into savings. First, in addition to banking the two-week paycheck, we added the monthly amount we would have paid our former landlord ($300) to the "New Home" savings account. Next, open a vacation account and deposit fifty dollars monthly into a bank in Virginia Beach, Virginia. This assured us of the additional funds needed for summer vacations and unforeseen emergencies. We decided to write down our spending on paper, which gave us a clearer picture of our spending. Part Two, Chapter Five, "Developing a Budget," will provide information on the process. Watching our bank accounts grow and having money to enjoy life's fun things made the sacrifice worthwhile.

In the Fall of 1990, we had over ten thousand dollars in the "New Home" savings account. By carefully managing our spending and savings in the interest-bearing checking account and vacation account, we managed to save over $13,000 and searched for a realtor. One realtor, impressed with our bank statements, suggested we purchase a house costing over $150,000, adjusted for inflation to a 2022 cost of $ 333,644.[10] My answer to the realtor was, "What's the use of purchasing the house sitting on the living room floor naked with no furniture?" Our thinking is that if either Diane or I lost employment, the other's income could continue to cover most of the monthly expenses while the other secures new employment. After considering twenty homes in February 1991, Diane, Benjamin, and I moved into a modestly priced home in a culturally mixed suburban neighborhood with an affordable mortgage.

For four years, things proceeded well. There were a few unexpected expenses, but we remained on course, with no significant debts and bills paid on time, despite facing the usual life challenges. However, three considerable life

---

[10] Calculate the Value of $150,000 in 1990. How much is it worth today? (dollartimes.com), 10.15.2022

challenges could have destroyed all we had achieved. In January 1995, I returned to complete my undergraduate studies at CUTS using a student loan. The loan was only for one year of education, but the amount to be repaid took much of the family's budget. By reinstituting the plan used to save for our home, we paid off the loan three years after graduation. The second was in 2003 when I suffered a heart attack. Though I was out of work for three months, the help of family savings, a sympathetic employer, and trusting friends sustained the family until my return. The third occurrence was in February 2006, when I was laid off from work. This proved to be the last full-time employment I would experience. Benjamin, now an adult, had moved out on his own. Diane continued to work. I received monthly unemployment compensation with marginal part-time employment. We still maintain a monthly mortgage, car note, and ongoing bills. The family struggled to decide the next steps for the next two years. When determining life's directions, it is best to seek the Lord. In the two years of praying and waiting, the Lord finally answered with instructions that, to me, did not make sense.

- **First**, **Attending Seminary**. The Lord directed me to apply. Graduating from an undergraduate college with a "Grade Point Average" of 2.04 did not seem likely to indicate that I would be admitted into an academic graduate program. I was wrong. I was admitted to Bethel Seminary of the East in September 2008 and graduated in 2011 with a 3.49 grade point average.

- **Second, Money for Seminary**. Seminary education is expensive. At the time, I was a fifty-eight-year-old man without full-time employment; how could I obtain the funds? As with my undergraduate studies, student loans would be the means. Unsure if I even qualified, I applied. Three weeks later, the loans were secure! As of this writing, I continue to repay by making timely monthly payments.

- **Third, "the Lord making a way out of no way."** Now accepted for seminary with a student loan, I still needed financial help. There was a thirty-year home mortgage and a car note to consider. However, the Lord saw that there would be no large debt to hinder my education. A thirty-year home mortgage and a new car loan were **paid**. By checking bank statements and years of savings, funds were available to pay off the home mortgage in nineteen years (December 2008); four months later, with the same funds, the loan for the 2003 new car was paid off. Both payoffs gave me the confidence to start and complete my education worry-free.

- **Fourth, Health Concerns**. I needed to be healthy to battle the rigors of seminary education. Years of being overweight left me with high blood pressure, diabetes, and heart disease. Feeling the burdens of seminary studies, the Lord gave wisdom for weight loss surgery. Losing one hundred and fifty pounds made me fit to overcome the health loads.

God is GOOD!

Although a graduate degree did not lead to full-time employment, it enabled the family to be more vigilant and watchful with our spending. Diane and I are officially retired, receiving Medicare, government pensions, and social security, and maintaining savings and retirement plans; we sustain a contented lifestyle. In 2020, during the height of COVID, another surprise. Our age, neighborhood changes, and the need to downsize caused us to look for a retirement home. Years of savings, settlement from a 2018 automobile accident, and an unexpected buyer who purchased our home ten days after listing made it possible to buy, in cash, a comfortable condominium unit. Though we are grateful for our savings and retirement incomes, we will continue to seek the Lord and be careful with spending as we wait for our deaths or His return. I say this because we are both confident that God will never forsake us. Numerous biblical scriptures encourage us that He (God) *will never leave nor forsake those who are His children.*[11] God proved this tremendous promise for Diane and me by placing a need through adopting a son and establishing financial peace. Chapter Two will show the structures to secure financial peace through a financial plan.

---

[11] Genesis 28:15; Deuteronomy 4:31; Deuteronomy 31:6,8; 1 Chronicles, 1 Corinthians 10:13; 2 Timothy 1:7; Hebrews 4:16; Hebrews 13:4-5 to name a few.

Chapter Two:

Psalms 20:4, *May he give you the desire of your heart and make all your plans succeed." - New International Version*

The "A-Team" was a television program that ran for five seasons from 1983 to 1987, depicting four fictional Army Veterans framed for a crime they did not commit while serving their country during the Vietnam War. The alleged crime is robbing the Bank of Hanoi and stealing millions of dollars. Each week's episode featured the team outwitting military police, escaping capture, and helping individuals abandoned and powerless due to political and social corruption. Later episodes show a government agency's use of the team performing covert or clandestine operations. The team comprises social misfits, such as Captain "Howling Mad Murdock, a supposedly psychotic but experienced air pilot played by Dwight Schultz, who is known for the Star Trek television and movie series. Lieutenant Templeton "Face Man" Peck, played by Dirk Benedict, who starred in the original Battlestar Galactica television and movie series, secured needed equipment by conning and trickery. Sergeant "BA" (Bad Attitude) Baracus[12], known for his menacing, intimidating physical physique, was played by "Mr. T" (born Laurence Tureaud), who also portrayed the boxer Clubber Lang in the 1982 film Rocky III. Their leader, Hannibal Smith, played by veteran television and movie actor George Peppard, had a

---

[12] "BA" sometimes referred to as "Bad Ass"

catchy phrase, "Love it when a plan comes together," used whenever the team successfully escaped capture or helped those in need, and a phrase that the Hicks Family would years later celebrate financial peace.

In chapter one, we saw God showing my family He was the source of financial peace. In this chapter, we will see how He structures a plan to achieve that financial peace. The plan is structured in a collection of ideas and concepts, taking time and effort to complete. It is a framework for security designed to overcome all financial challenges while building comfort and maintaining financial peace.

The structure of any plan holds it together, allowing it time to succeed. As a verb, the word structure is defined as *"a construct or arrangement according to a plan...* [13] Structures are found in computer technology, art, government, law, and education, to name a few. The structure is necessary for the life and success of any plan. For the Hicks family financial plan, the structures supporting the plan were found in four singular supporting constructions...***Vision***, ***Responsibility***, ***Support***, and ***Trust.***

---

[13] structure definition - Search (bing.com)

These four made the Hicks family's financial picture clear, understandable, workable, and healthy. Let's view each supporting structure.

Vision! *"Where there is no vision, the people perish.[14]*

King Solomon, the ancient king of Israel, is renowned for his wise words, which inspire, impart knowledge, and offer hope. His words of vision were also used by the noted French entrepreneur and political visionary Jean Monnet (born November 9, 1888, died March 16, 1979). He is considered one of the founders of the European Union, pioneering European Unity.[15] However, the words have been misunderstood and used as an incentive in developing a missionary or vision statement that expresses the directions of groups, such as churches, corporations, and countries, as they navigate towards a successful and fruitful existence. Nevertheless, in a biblical sense, it refers to a unique vision or revelation from the Lord. This revelation prevents devastation and decay if not followed precisely.

---

[14] [14] Proverbs 29:18, King James Version
[15] Jean Monnet - Wikipedia, November 29, 2022

Diane and I needed a clear vision to devise a plan for financial peace. Like in all things, we were powerless but motivated, had intelligence but lacked experience, and were willing to make sacrifices but did not know where to start. As stated in Chapter One, the vision was directed by God through the words of Herb Denenberg, an experienced man of financial knowledge and insight. Mr. Denenberg gave a very frank and candid description of our inadequate financial condition. Our desires and good intentions were directed toward our son Benjamin's welfare and life. When we learn that a down payment of one hundred dollars to secure a home fell short, the Lord convicted our hearts to follow the visionary words of Mr. Denenberg. Words of sound advice provide light, lighting the way. Even now, Mr. Denenberg's words continue to aid us as new financial challenges arise for the family. We found that all financial plans must start with a vision, not from the human heart or mind. But from the Lord.

Responsibility! *"Too many cooks spoil the broth[i].*

With the vision in place, Diane and I realized we were responsible for its implementation. The word responsibility became another support structure to consider. The word, defined as "the state or fact of having a duty to

deal with something or having control over someone,*"16*
became our watchword. Knowing the responsibilities ahead
of us, we were unsure how they might play out in their
implementation. Pondering the answer, we concluded that
though the plan involved the two of us, there needed to be
an accountable person or a "head cook." The phrase "too
many cooks spoil the broth" was coined in 1575 by George
Gascoigne, an English poet said to be "the most important
poet in the early Elizabethan era."[17] The saying suggests
that if many people and personalities take leadership in an
action, the greater the possibility that the action will fail.
Though Diane and I agreed to the plan, we soon discovered
that we had differing ideas on how to move forward. For
example, disagreements arose when discussing which of
our biweekly payroll checks should be deposited in the
"New Home" account. We knew that the Lord was the
ultimate overseer of our plan; we needed someone to be His
single physical instrument. Though a single physical
instrument, there were standards we both agreed must be
practiced.

---

[16] responsibility definition - Search (bing.com), 23/23/2024
[17] George Gascoigne - Wikipedia 12/6/2019

First, the head cook must not act with the attitude of an aggressive, commanding military leader. Nor as a ruthless chief executive officer (CEO) of a large corporation bent on controlling corporate interest. Neither my wife, Diane, nor I want to feel enslaved or managed by the other. We have seen families controlled by dominating personalities, leading to dysfunctional family dynamics. This type of head cook leading the family would not please the Lord or promote the family's financial peace. **Next,** the head cook does not need to be a genius. In his book, "Hidden Habits of Genius," Craig Wright, Ph.D., author, notes that being a genius is not equal to being an intellectual giant." "*Intellectual giants are often curious people.*[18] *They love to pick things apart to see how they work...*[19] One does not need to earn a Master of Business Administration (MBA) or show years of experience serving in a financial institution. Being curious opens the door to investigating all possible financial strategies available to the family. This approach presents numerous financial possibilities to consider. And **lastly,** a head cook is willing to include the immediate family before making financial

---

[18] 4 Reasons Why Curiosity Is Important and How to Develop It - LifeHack, 9.1
2023
[19] 15 Traits of a Genius Person - New Kids Center, 9.1.2023

decisions. Everyone must be aware of what's happening in the process. Though other family members are not involved in the day-to-day operations, monthly meetings give information to keep the family informed and the head cook honest. (More information on this subject will be discussed in Chapter Three). Feelings of inclusion, not exclusion, are experienced when others are brought into the process. It is like I learn in seminary. A seminary degree, or any higher learning degree, does not prove superiority over others. Do not discount family members who did not attend an institution of higher learning or complete a higher learning degree. Though they may not have completed a degree, they have life experiences. Seek them out as one would seek information from a library. After much more discussion and prayer, it was agreed that the head cook would be me. However, I continue to lean on my wife, Diane, my "Sous chef.".

Support: *"Where there is no counsel, the people fall; but there is safety in the multitude of counselors...*[20]

With a head cook secured and family members involved, it was imperative to *invite* trustworthy, experienced, and financially responsible individuals. These

---

[20] Proverbs 11:14

are not additional head cooks, but those who provide counsel. The above statement from King Solomon expresses two significant thoughts about seeking counsel from experienced people. **First,** it is God's will to provide His people with multitudes of counselors with experience to give guidance and leadership. God wants His people to have all the tools they need to live a life of security and peace. In matters of finances, having multiple counselors brings the same security and peace. Seek counselors with firsthand knowledge, years of education, proficiency, and familiarity with financial planning issues. There is safety in bringing the opinions of multiple counselors. Not one person knows everything about every area of the economic system. We can thank God that He has equipped many with financial knowledge and skills. **Next,** having a multitude of counselors allows one to weigh all opinions before finalizing a plan. Since the Hicks' financial plan would be the family's most critical, it was essential to consider all financial options before deciding. **Finally**, many counselors give support, bringing stability and timely resources as sounding boards to bounce off ideas, broad shoulders to cry on, and confidence that one is not alone. Below is a summary list of the people a head cook must look to when making critical financial decisions.

- Husbands, Wives, Significant Others: My wife Diane brought me back to a level place when I rose beyond myself, keeping me focused on the financial goals ahead.
- Seniors, not necessarily in age, but in experience. Those who tackled the many financial challenges while experiencing both victories and defeats.
- Financial Advisors are those knowledgeable in areas where the responsible person lacks knowledge. My American Heritage Federal Credit Union advisor helped me understand investment trends, market strengths, weaknesses, and market strategies. I will speak more about advisors in Chapter Six.

Trust: *"But Jesus beheld them, and said unto them, with men this is impossible, but with God all things are possible.[21]"*

A story I have heard many times explains a pastor asking his congregation to stand up from their seats and then asking them to sit. Immediately, the pastor exclaimed that no one had checked whether their chairs were stable or

---

[21] King James Bible, Matthew 19:26

if their chairs could support their weight. Trust is needed in all financial endeavors. I am not speaking about relying entirely on an economic system or a human being. It is trusting, depending entirely on God. For with God, all things are possible. The Bible contains examples of God "making a way out of no way," healing broken bodies and souls while restoring physical and spiritual life.

When our son Benjamin came into our lives, we realized the need to trust the Lord. We could not live the next ten or more years of marriage as we did the first ten. We were not living alone. Benjamin's life was now our responsibility. As an infant, he was unable to fend for himself. His future depended on our success. We did not want him to grow up without a strong, healthy financial plan. Our trust in the Lord was determined by our willingness to submit to the following...

- **All things belong to God:** Diane and I submitted to the financial outcome established by God. Regardless of the outcome, though the work may not be what we desired, the result would be completed to God's satisfaction and glory. And whatever God requires, we will benefit from it.

- **God is the provider of all things.** No one else has the resources to reach a successful financial conclusion. We could not depend on political or governmental programs. Programs change as new political parties are voted in and when new government policies are enacted. In addition, we cannot rely solely on financial institutions, interest rates, stock markets, or banks, as they can become unstable. Only the Lord can and will provide us with all things.

- **Sacrificing selfish desires and wants.** We decrease for the Lord to increase.[22] Our desires and wants take second place to those of the Lord. We become slaves (a word many do not like) to His will and ways, having our hearts and minds under His complete control.

- **Listening and Following.** Seeking and receiving instructions and encouragement from the Lord through the Bible. God's word helps us tackle all of life's issues. It does not work unless one opens and seriously reads the Bible, listens to its biblical

---

[22] John 3:30, He must increase, but I must decrease." Words spoken by John the Baptist to give meaning that his ministry was to proclaim Jesus Christ, not himself.

truths, and obeys it by following its powerful directions.

The Hicks financial plan continues to be a work in progress. I can say that with each challenge, each roadblock, and each detour, with breath still in our bodies, Diane and I will trust God. Trusting God has proven that, over the past forty years since we began the plan, Diane and I have testified of the Lord's goodness, grace, love, and mercy upon our lives. Benjamin has long left home, living independently and facing financial challenges. We continue to experience a mixture of victories and defeats, but the economic plan continues to work. It is a continual testimony of our Lord's grace and mercy upon this family, and His vision regarding our finances is becoming an everlasting reality. That is why we can now say, **"We love it when a plan comes together!"**

In Chapter Three, we will examine the financial health of the Hicks' financial plan, guided by the Lord, as the family establishes a firm economic foundation for financial peace.

Chapter Three:

Building a Firm
Foundation

Psalms 127:1, "*Unless the L*ORD *builds a house, its builders labor over it in vain; unless the L*ORD *watches over a city, the watchman stays alert in vain." -God's Word Translation.*

In the spring of 1964, at the age of ten, I accepted Jesus Christ as my Lord and Savior during a Sunday school assembly meeting at the Corinthian Baptist Church in Philadelphia, Pennsylvania. God used the late Deacon George W. Lee, Sr. (Sunday School Superintendent), under the direction of the late Pastor M.W. Newsome, and his band of dedicated teachers to open my mind and heart to the gospel of salvation. Up to that time, I attended countless funerals for loved ones, relatives, and friends. Worried and concerned about my immortality, I desired assurance of life after death. Accepting Jesus, the living Word of God,[23] gave me that assurance. It is the foundation that continues to uphold my faith and existence. A song that comes to mind is one that was sung during Sunday School. The song "How Firm a Foundation." The unknown composer speaks of a spiritual foundation found by faith in Jesus Christ. The lyric to the first stanza below gives testimony to that foundation...

"How firm a foundation, ye saints of the Lord,
is laid for your faith in His excellent word!
What more can He say than to you He hath said-

---

[23] John 1:14

To you who for refuge to Jesus have fled."[24]

Rocks are used as firm structural foundations. They are a naturally occurring mass or collection of raw mineral materials used to build sturdy structures for centuries. The minerals recovered by its mining include precious metals and stones. Ancient Egyptians used dates from 4000 BCE. Around 2800 BCE, Mongolians began constructing *military* fortifications. Ancient Romans used rocks for bridges and buildings.[25] Though modern use is limited to building materials like steel, cement, and concrete, it is still popular as a strong building material.[26]

In the Sermon on the Mount, chapters 5-7, Jesus Christ speaks of a firm foundation in the parable of two builders.[27] I imagine these skillful builders erected houses sincerely intending to support themselves and their families. There were no indications that both houses were temporary structures or that there were plans for the builders to relocate their families later. One builder, Jesus,

---

[24] How Firm a Foundation > Lyrics | Anonymous/Unknown (timelesstruths.org), 1/18/2024
[25] Rock (geology) - Wikipedia, 12/8/2022
[26] Rock (geology) - Wikipedia October 15, 2022
[27] Matthew 7: 24-28

called "wise," built his house on a rock foundation. When natural disasters, such as rain, floods, winds, and storms, beat against his house, it stood firm and could withstand. However, the other builder, Jesus, referred to as "foolish," built his house on sand. When these same natural disasters struck his home, the house collapsed due to its porous foundation.

Chapter One of this book highlights the importance of developing financial peace. Chapter Two explains the structures for establishing a plan to sustain that peace. This chapter of Jesus' account of the two builders gives my family an example of maintaining financial peace with a firm economic foundation. It would be foolish to think that natural disasters, in the form of life challenges, will not arise. Challenges will arise. As Jesus speaks of rocks functioning as strong building materials in constructing a firm foundation for a house, building a solid financial foundation starts with suitable building materials. Strong materials are portrayed by the wise builder as durable while offering peace, protection, and security. The materials that provide a firm structure and foundation for the Hicks Family's financial plan are based on the materials I call *"Carve, Convene, and Custody."*

Carve! (The Family Budget)

Since the dawn of civilization, humans have used sharp instruments to create surfaces for drawing thoughts and ideas, which have been interpreted both privately and publicly. It started with the use of sticks, drawing ideas in dirt. Then, picture drawings were chiseled on rocks using metal instruments. Later, the use of plants to produce ink and paper simplified the process, eventually leading to the development of the printing press, which enabled the production of books and manuals. The invention of the typewriter simplified and made more profitable the public's access to manufacturing; later, computers opened doors to the internet, where thoughts were transported throughout the earth. Some speculate that the next step will not be in written form but in words transmitted from one human consciousness to another.

It is essential to carve writing thoughts, concepts, dreams, and facts on paper. It can make one feel better, help one remember, and make healthier decisions while setting goals. These and other reasons are valuable and useful. The adage "a picture is worth a thousand words" means that a single image can convey multiple ideas. For the Hicks Family, it highlighted the importance of documenting personal, detailed financial information in writing, providing insight into how money is obtained and dispersed. The detailed, picturesque portrait showing where the Hicks funds were received and disbursed is called a **"Budget."**

Diane and I have seen and experienced the constructive worth of a church budget for ministry as church leaders. It is a path financially accountable churches travel to meet their many financial obligations and responsibilities. Similarly, budgets are also used within private and public businesses. We asked, "Why not for family use?" A simple family budget was produced with an electric typewriter. I will now share how the budget was developed.

As seen in *Figure #1,* each expense, which identifies family spending, was categorized as a "Line Item" to track spending. A line item is an itemized appropriation of what was and would be spent monthly within a budget.[28]

---

[28] Line-item Definition & Meaning - Merriam-Webster, October 15, 2022

Figure #1 Spending Category

Items	Month 1	Month 2	Month 3
NECESSITIES			
Childcare			
Utilities			
Groceries	$150	$185	$225
Church Offerings			
Credit Cards			
Life Insurance			
Health Insurance			
Auto Insurance			
Auto Fuel			
Household Needs			
Cable			
ENTERTAINMENT			
Vacations/Day Trips			
Others			
PERSONAL			
Spouse One			
Spouse Two			

The initial budget (1989 to 1990) that Diane and I listed included only the family's monthly expenses for the budgeted year. Our reasoning was based on our belief that irresponsible spending was the reason for financial instability. Three months into the budget, we noticed that the budget did not show responsible spending. For example, shown again in *Figure #1*, groceries had the highest spending in the first month. For the second month, the family's expenditure was higher than in the first month. Then, in the third month, grocery spending was higher again. Concerned that the family was spending more on groceries than other line items, I reviewed our spending habits, which confirmed that spending was being taken away from different areas. The obvious answer was to reduce spending. Though this was an answer, I saw it as a bandage covering a financial wound, but not bringing financial peace. As I looked for an answer, it was at arm's length in the form of the family's income. Income from payroll, gifts, tax returns, and ministry is designed to help control family spending.

Figure #2 Income.

Item	Monthly	Yearly
PAYROLL		
Spouse One		
Spouse Two		
OTHER INCOME		
Gifts from Others		
Tax Returns		
Ministry Gifts		

Income is the money to pay for the items in the spending category. Without it, there would be no savings or spending. In addition, income can tell what you must spend and how it should be spent. Also, it stops unnecessary expenditure. For example, if one has potential spending totaling $500 and one's income is also $500, one has sufficient income to fulfill the spending requirement. If the income is less than the expected expenses, one must either increase or reduce spending. In addition, having more income than what is spent is profit used for savings. Recording on paper gave me the pictographic view needed to handle the family finances properly. In the fourth month, we list both spending and income. *Figure #11,* Part Two of the book, shows a sample of the corrected first budget. We are grateful this mistake did not hinder the budget process.

Tracking spending and income enabled the determination of spending habits that would help adjust monthly family spending habits while considering the following year's budget. It proved to be the foundation for all future budgets. Carving a budget was the first financial building block to establish that firm economic foundation. Chapter Five will provide a detailed explanation of budget creation. However, the second financial building material proved to be as important.

Convene! (The Family Meeting)

The Hicks Family's budget is a financial tool providing information on income and spending. Though an excellent tool, it lacks a platform for family members to receive answers to meaningful and essential questions. To find a solution, I looked within my workplace. There, employees receive written information from their employer about the tasks they must perform. The employer would meet with the employee throughout their employment to review and discuss the performance task issues. To promote a good workplace, these meetings allowed employees and the employer opportunities to express their thoughts and opinions openly. The meeting outcomes may not have satisfied everyone in attendance, but the meetings provided helpful and valuable information. Hence, the establishment of the Hicks' family, **Family Meeting**.

Diane, Benjamin (who was old enough and lived in the home), and I met monthly to discuss family business. Meetings started with prayer. Minutes from the last meeting were read, and the accuracy and approval were agreed upon, followed by the discussion of financials. Financials examined monthly spending and its impact on the yearly budget. If monthly spending became out of hand, corrections were discussed. Suppose the monthly expenditure was less than the budgeted amount. As explained earlier in the chapter, if profit is made, it is placed in savings. There were times when specific spending needs were addressed. For example, a washing machine became a spending need. It was hard, with a young child, to spend hours at a community laundromat. In June 1989, my job handed out end-of-business-year bonuses, which provided money for a washing machine. However, the washing machine still weighed against other pressing family needs. After discussing and agreeing on the need, the family sought the best price. A washing machine was purchased. Later in the year, family meetings discussed replacing a porch roof, and then the basement steps. Every new year, the family faced new obstacles that could strain the budget. In addition to the family budget, non-budget issues were discussed. Most discussions centered on family issues, including vacation plans, school, and relationships, while at other times, the focus shifted to community, national, and world events.

Meetings would be no longer than sixty minutes, and later increase to ninety minutes. Before the meeting ended, and if more time was needed, fifteen to twenty minutes were added upon agreement by all. If issues were still unresolved, they were set aside for discussion at a later meeting. Meetings always ended with the scheduling of the following month's meeting and prayer. This meeting format continues.

"Meeting Notes," later called the "**Agenda,**" were vital, for they were not only a chronicle listing of items discussed but also assignments given to family members to complete before the next meeting. All notes were filed away to be referred to as needed. Once purchased, notes were saved to a computer file, replacing paper copies. A sample of a typical family's agenda can be found below.

Meeting Notes (Agenda) *Figure #3*

Hicks Family Meeting for March 1990

Opening Prayer

- **Reading the minutes of last month's meeting (Accepted or Rejected)**
- **Financial Report**:
    - *Review the family budget*
    - *Last month's income and spending*
    - *Upcoming significant spending/income*
    - *Adjustments to the budget*
- **Church Issues**
- **Family Issues**
- **Rest and Restoration**
    - *Monthly Family Outing*
    - *Monthly Date Night*
- **New Business**
- **Scheduling of Next Meeting**
- **Closing Prayer**

Each meeting allowed family members to meet as equals, discussing whatever was on their minds. Lively discussions were encouraged, allowing family members to feel comfortable bringing up sensitive issues. Though not every meeting ended in agreement, it can be safely said that no one felt disrespected. The third financial building material proved equally significant, and the family could not live without it.

Custody! (The Family Ownership)

Carving a robust and durable budget and having the means to convene with family members alone could not stand together. Taking custody of the budget would. My wife Diane and I experienced this in adopting our son Benjamin. After ten years of marriage, Diane and I felt empty. We tried naturally to have children. We conferred with Obstetricians and tried various methods and practices without success. We had thought about adoption before marriage, but not as a primary source for parenting. Entering the eleventh year of marriage without children, thoughts of parenting became unimportant as Diane settled on her career and I on earning an undergraduate degree. But God decided to make parenting imperative to our lives. As a college student, I worked part-time at a Christian elementary and secondary school, serving as a substitute teacher and driver for elementary school students. While transporting students to and from school, I had little conversation except for timely instructions on travel safety.

While I drove, the students watched the surroundings from the vehicle windows or talked amongst themselves. This one day was different. Not remembering what caused the question, a ten-year-old female student asked me, **"Mr. Hicks, do you have any children?"** Not going into detail, I answered, "The Lord has not blessed me or my wife." Thinking the subject closed, I was surprised. The very next day, while picking up the students from their homes, the mother of the student who asked the question came running to the school vehicle with a photo and said, "You must adopt this child!" It was a photograph of Benjamin. This started a series of steps that led Benjamin to be part of the family. The lesson learned became the third financial building material of the Hicks financial foundation.

What is the lesson learned? My wife Diane and I approach the need to succeed with determination to sustain a healthy financial foundation, just as we did with the adoption process. As the definition of custody explains, we took *"immediate charge and control, exercising authority and safekeeping."*[29] Of the financial structure established by the Lord. Let me share three words from the above definition that best describe the process.

---

[29] custody - Search (bing.com)

Immediate: Receiving the vision given by the Lord through Herb Denenberg, Diane and I promptly took ownership. For us, it did not make sense to wait. With Benjamin being a part of our lives, the Lord gave us the means, conviction, directions, wisdom, and plan. By not delaying, we witness the Lord providing a home, steady employment, and financial accounts. As earlier stated, there were challenges, but they were survivable. Following all the Lord brought to our attention, we march forward, refusing to look back. **Authority:** Diane and I were given authority to manage the outcome. A biblical example is found in the ministry of the Apostle Paul. He exclaimed on return from his first missionary journey to the Christian church Council in Jerusalem, made up of Jewish Christians, where he was given authority to proclaim the message of salvation in Christ as a "minister of the Gentiles."[30] Led by the Lord, Paul made two additional missionary journeys: one back to those gentile nations he visited during the first and then to the city of Rome. Diane and I were given the authority to do this excellent task. We took ownership and determined to see it through. We sought to strengthen our control by refining the financial plan. This was achieved through reading financial journals, seeking sound advice

---

[30] Acts 15:4-41

from others, and exercising careful spending habits. We continue to rely on God's guidance and power, knowing, as the Apostle Paul did, that we will be successful.

Safekeeping: Protecting the financial plan daily, then weekly, and monthly, watching the plan mature after eighteen months to see it continue today, and protecting it from the challenges that life brings. As stated in Chapter One, the challenges were complex, but we knew we needed to follow through to succeed. We were always diligent in exercising restraint, not deviating from the plan, and not allowing outside forces to disrupt the structure. These were found in the challenges of life. The physical challenges that arise from desiring things not included in the goals. Additionally, there are the spiritual challenges of wishing to follow and please God and being tempted to turn to ungodly pleasures, as well as the emotional difficulties of sacrificing many deep and embedded desires. There were hurtful challenges found among the few who did not support our efforts. Though they said they were keeping my family in their prayers, I felt some viewed our actions as folly. One example was the person boldly telling me that the family's effort would fail. He reasoned that the cost to the family was too high in terms of time, sacrifice, the economy, and forces beyond our control. Diane and I refuse to succumb, pressing forward.

"On Jesus Christ, I stand; all other ground is sinking sand; all other ground is sinking sand."[31] Chorus from another Sunday School song. The Hicks Family's financial peace stands only because of our firm foundation built with the building materials of **Crave, Convene**, and **Custody** orchestrated by Jesus Christ. I can't entirely agree with those promoting a financial foundation apart from Jesus Christ, despite their good intentions. Whether governmental, social, public, or institutional, I must add even religious leaders. Unfortunately, some of these institutions and religious leaders have led many into financial ruin. They are like the foolish builders found in Matthew Chapter Seven. As the wise builder of the same chapter, seek suitable building materials found in Christ Jesus to hold up against life's challenges. Only Jesus Christ can blend the right ingredients, creating a foundation where a healthy financial structure can succeed, promoting peace. I say again that the suitable building materials for a firm

---

[31] Song, "My Hope is Built on Nothing Else," lyrics by Edward Mote (1797-1874), music by William Bradbury (1816-1868), Assurance and Joy of Salvation.

foundation are found in Jesus Christ. Amen! Chapter Four will testify to people God gave me to supplement my understanding, leading to a peaceful financial plan.

Chapter Four:

Frame of
References

Hebrews 12:1, *Therefore, having so vast a cloud of witnesses surrounding us, and throwing off everything that hinders us and especially the sin that so easily entangles us, let us keep running with endurance the race set before us,-* International Standard Version (ISV)

"Frame of References" is a term I studied as an undergraduate at the Center for Urban Theological Studies (CUTS). It's a study that has assisted me as I journeyed towards financial peace. The term was coined by Carl Rogers (1902-1987), a noted psychologist and founder of person-centered therapy. A frame of reference is a *"set of criteria or stated values in relationship to measurements or judgments made."*[32] These criteria, or "life experiences," are shaped by what is learned or experienced by words or deeds. Knowing a client's frame of reference provides insight into the life events that shape the themes of a person's present condition. It helps the therapist understand existing emotional issues, for they project the person's worth and introjected values, leading towards sound treatment. However, the therapist must be careful not to inject their frame of reference but act as a companion to the client, entering their frame of reference and viewing life as the client considers it.[33] Carl Rogers used this type of counseling to find the foundation that troubled the troubled mind.

---

[32] What is the definition of a frame of reference? - Search (bing.com),3.27.2023
[33] Ibid,2.7.2023

The CUTS class emphasizes that frames of reference are personal, natural, or unnatural occurrences of life event points. These life events points can be both positive and negative. A negative example can be found in an individual who was abused as a child and is living a present life, harming others. An individual with a positive trait is one whose parents perform charitable works, and now they are doing the same. In establishing and maintaining a healthy financial picture, negative and positive life points shape my present economic state. My negative life points are evident in the mistakes I've made along the way. These were mistakes made due to personal setbacks, the avoidance of potentially rewarding opportunities, or poor decision-making. My positive life points were found in men who were determined to provide for their loved ones despite a lack of education or discouragement from others, but were determined to overcome all and achieve. All God gave me to experience, proving his concern for me while shaping my development of a peaceful financial life.

Chapter One highlighted the importance of developing financial peace. Chapter Two explained the structures for establishing a plan to sustain that peace.

Chapter Three explained the importance of maintaining financial peace with a firm economic foundation. This chapter will show how the many frames of reference have made me realize my full economic potential, leading to financial peace.

Negative Life Points...Mistakes
"The man who makes no mistakes does not usually make anything."[34]

Edward John Phelps, "19th-century lawyer and diplomat from the state of Vermont,"[35] Words I came to treasure. I found living in a world where making mistakes was foolish and destructive. As a young child, I watched movies where the hero used the villain's own mistakes to lead to the villain's defeat. In the classroom, it was not emotionally healthy to make mistakes. I mistakenly used the wrong verb tense in several sentences in a high school English writing class. The teacher showed my work in class as an example of poor writing skills. His actions led me to maintain poor writing habits, which persist to this day. Thank God for editors. The news media reports the

---

[34] The New Encyclopedia of Christian Quotations, pg. 676, Compiled by Mark Water, Baker Books, Grand Rapids, MI 1984
[35] Edward John Phelps - Wikipedia

mistakes in politics, sports, businesses, and companies. These reports cause those making a mistake to face public embarrassment and, sometimes, social ruin. But as I ponder the words of Edward John Phelps, mistakes are actions made towards a goal. Mistakes make the goal attainable because one can examine the errors causing the mistake, thus deciding to correct, improve, or take another action. The Hicks family has made mistakes in the quest for financial peace. To list the many mistakes made as the family strives toward financial peace, I would need to write another book on the subject. Instead, let me give two examples: one personal and the other from my business experience, which brought success.

I am a man of faith. I have written about how my family and I place our faith and love for God. How God brought and continues to move toward financial peace is a testimony of his love, mercy, and grace upon us. My mistake was keeping God out of my life for nine years. It began after the death of my mother, Grace Hicks. Emotionally, it hit me hard. Praise the Lord, I did not disband the family; however, I separated myself from God. I continue to be true to the needs of the family. I kept gainful employment and oversaw family finances.

However, I stopped preaching, praying, reading the Bible, and attending church. Though *"holy church members"* tried to convince my wife, Diane, to leave me, she remained faithful to me by praying and trusting God. She was convinced that whenever I returned to faith, *"I would be better than before."* During the nine years I call my dark passage, the Lord never took His hands from me. He desires to bring me back in fellowship with him. This proof is found in the Bible verse Revelation 3:20, **"Behold, I stand at the door, and knock: if any man hears my voice, and open the door, I will come into him, and sup with him, and he with me**.[36] Lessons learned from my nine-year mistake gave me a new appreciation of God. It shows my standing in the presence of his greatness. Lesson learned: I can lead the family towards financial peace if I remember that it is not I, but the God I trust. Diane was right; I became better.

An automobile purchased out of selfishness is a business example of making a mistake. There needed to be more than a reliable automobile. The family must have a second. The first is to travel for relaxation and fun, the second for business. The auto chosen was owned by what

---

[36] King James Bible

the family thought was a friend. He formerly worked for our local government and claimed faith in God. As I examined the vehicle, he quoted Bible verses and spoke of faithful radio ministers. I should have become suspicious when he only allowed me to drive the car three blocks around his home, stating that the vehicle did not have proper auto tags to identify ownership. Liking the auto, I quickly agreed to the sale. Three thousand dollars, and two weeks later, I own a vehicle needing significant repairs. I sold it to a family friend for scraps. Lesson learned: though the mistake of purchasing the car was embarrassing, emotionally draining, and made me feel like a fool, it made me not think with my feelings but with my head. Yes, it was good to have a second vehicle. It was better to purchase a car after careful examination. The examination included the vehicle, the source (where it came from), and the actual need. Understanding the need to examine served me well as I tackled planned and unplanned financial situations. Mistakes are like book notes to life; learn from them and use them as valuable resources.

As you continue to read, I will devote more time and effort to the positive life events. Not that the negatives were less critical, for they were not. The positive life events echo louder. In this book, several positive life events established my present reality toward financial peace. They included the adoption of son Benjamin. With its many welfare liens, the house enabled my family to live (rent-free) until a home was secure, and Radio personality Herb Denenberg with his wise counsel. Properly acknowledging these and other events within the pages of this book would be impossible. However, I wish to credit two life event points I believe the Lord used mightily, a blessing to my family and hopefully to you, the reader.

"Positive Life Forces" (Determination, Men of the Hicks Family)

1 Corinthians 9:24 (KJV) *Know ye not that they run in a race, all run, but one receives the prize? So run, that ye may obtain.*

I am the first child and son of the marriage of Otis Benjamin Hicks, Senior, and Grace Virginia Miller. Born during the Civil Rights Movement, I had firsthand experience of the shame and embarrassment of America. My mother tells how, at age four, I contributed positively to the movement. Riding in a car with my parents to my father's family home in Oxford, North Carolina, we stopped at a drug store in Richmond, Virginia, so my mother could purchase a comb. The store had a lunch counter that served only white people. I was hungry and smelling cooked food. I ran to its counter, climbed into a seat, and banged on the counter, repeatedly saying, "I WANT TO EAT." My mother quickly dragged me away. I don't know if she had time to purchase the comb. Though this and other experiences framed my response to racism, it also helped prepare my response to finances because I carried the genes of determination inherited by the men of the Hicks family.

For as long as I can remember, I have heard the statement, *"Son, why don't you pay yourself first?* I interpreted the words to mean that whenever I received a paycheck for hard labor, I should set aside a portion of the money and spend it on myself immediately. After hearing it again, I realized I should save, not spend. I was told that the saying goes back to the early days after American Slavery, when black parents in the South would encourage their children to save. These parents realized that achieving financial success was the key to survival in a predominantly white-dominated world. I remember my father and mother telling stories of senior relatives and friends saving coins in mason jars and locked metal boxes buried in the ground around their homes or hiding paper money sewn inside or under mattresses. My great-grandfather Edmond Hicks may not have saved coins in mason jars or under mattresses; he was determined to obtain all known financial resources so his family could fulfill their hopes and dreams.

Edmond Hicks was born in 1859, under slavery, the son of Sedrick and Fannie Hicks. There is no information about whether he had brothers or sisters or the outcomes of his father, Sedrick, or mother, Fannie. In 1865, he and his parents were free. It was reported that he could not read or write. He married twice, once to Marie Crews, and the union produced three children. Upon her death, he married Emily Francis Herndon, with whom eight children were born; my grandfather, Thurston Hicks, came from this union. In 1895, Edmond purchased a hundred acres of land from a former enslaver in Oxford, Granville County, North Carolina. There, he became a prosperous farmer growing tobacco. By the turn of the century, Edmond would purchase another hundred acres of land in Southerland, Virginia.[37] He would die in 1938 at the age of 79; however,

---

[37] Develop for Hicks Family Reunion, July 5, 2003

he faithfully, tirelessly, sacrificially, and with determination supported his family, of which I am a beneficiary.

Thurston Hicks, my grandfather, was the son of Edmond Hicks, born in 1903. What I know about him comes from my many visits to the farm he inherited from his father in Oxford, North Carolina. And what I heard others say about him. His story is impressive for a black man living during Jim Crow.[38]   I was told he was a respected man. This respect was earned by hard work, support for his community, determination, and caring for his family, including his wife Rose, sons Thomas, Otis (my father), and William. I came to know him from that farm. Every year, from age four to sixteen, my brother (Charles), sisters (Sylvia, Shelia, and Sharon), and I spent a week on the farm. It did not have indoor plumbing, but an outhouse (outdoor privy) and a clean water well. It had indoor electricity, a wood-burning stove, and good food. We picked tobacco leaves, fruits, and vegetables, fed the hogs, collected eggs and milk cows, rode mules, and swam in the

---

[38] Jim Crow, period of American History from the end of Reconstruction 1877 till the mid-20th century where laws written supporting racial segregation and discrimination. Mostly practices in southern states.

nearby creek while enjoying the quiet and beauty of the land. It is a testament to the determination, hard work, and collaborative skills that made my grandfather successful. This formula added to my frame of reference, which serves me well.

Otis Hicks Senior, my father, born in 1925, took the above scriptural text to heart. He believed in having a healthy, strong financial foundation; I sadly realized this after his death. This is amazing for a man with an eighth-grade education. Supporting a family of six, he worked three jobs. From Mondays to Fridays, he left home early in the morning to return in the early evening, leaving after dinner for the second job. On Saturdays, he worked half days and then went for his third job or performed odd jobs around the neighborhood. Sundays, he rested. Not only did he work, but he also saved. He kept money in the bank for household and family needs. He held the additional cash in a safe, which I learned later as a young adult. He built the safe into a wall in the basement of his family home. I believe the term "holding a dollar until it hollers" was his motto. I remember when he argued with my mother about purchasing gym shoes for me. He wanted the shoes from Woolworths (a five-and-dime store). The shoes, called

Bobo's,[39] They were cheaply made, costing two dollars. My mother insists on purchasing from Sears and Roebuck's, known today as Sears Discount Store. The shoes were of higher quality, costing five dollars. I thank God my mother won. Although holding two or more jobs robbed me of a personal relationship with him, as an adult with a son, I now understand. The above scripture states that Otis Hicks Senior ran life's race determined not just to survive. He ran the race so that his children would not face ridicule, scorn, or unhappiness of living unproductive lives. His children did not grow up to be college professors, doctors, or lawyers. They grew up to become responsible and respectful people, guided by the knowledge that hard work yields good things. My great-grandfather, grandfather, and father are the positive life events that have influenced my financial condition and shaped my future. Self-determination was not the only example of positive frames of reference. Actions are equally important, as seen in my final example.

---

[39] "An imitation of something, particularly a well-known product, usually lower in quality than the original.

Positive Life Forces (Actions, "The Man from Zimbabwe")

"We serve a great big wonderful God; we serve a great big wonderful God. A God who's always victorious, always watching over us, a great big wonderful God."

The above words are chronicled and recorded into many Christian songs and titles, and were first introduced to me in 1973 by a brilliant, faithful man of God. A man from the African country of Rhodesia, now known as the Republic of Zimbabwe, was living alone in this country. The song is a testimony of the goodness of God upon his life. He first experienced this as God brought him to this country to study for the ministry at the academically prestigious Philadelphia College of Bible, now named Cairn University. College life, though demanding, did not hinder him from completing a bachelor's degree and then later a master's degree. As a fellow student, I found him diligent in his studies, dedicating hours and days to them. In addition, he was engaged in his employment. He took on two, sometimes three jobs. I thought it was to supplement his college and living expenses. I later learned that it would be the second experience of the song, where I would witness the goodness of God and hear a testimony on handling personal finances.

He lived a simple life. I never saw him splurge for anything. Whatever he purchased was for the necessities of life. I thought he owned two or three suits. He owned one, which he kept in immaculate condition. He wore the suit to class, on the job, for leisure, and to church. He enjoyed going out for meals with friends. He said it allowed him to escape the monotony of college cafeteria food. I remember inviting him to my home for dinner one Friday evening. My mother, a former Roman Catholic, continues the tradition of meatless Fridays. Friday's menu consists of fried potatoes with onions and peas, baked fish for my father, and fried fish sticks for my brother and three sisters. When he ate the fish sticks, he exclaimed, "It tastes like steak."

Though studying and working were necessary for him to stay in this country, I learned that saving was used for another project. His savings would make it possible to bring him the love of his life to become his wife. Weekly, without fail, he deposits his employment income into a local savings bank account. As he saved, he kept a calendar on the wall of his dorm room. The calendar gave him a visual picture, each day marked with an x, fixing his mind on the days remaining until her arrival. In addition, as the arrival time grew near, the calendar prompted him to purchase her airfare and cover her expenses. As we met, he reported the days until her arrival. Seeing him faithfully save his hard-earned money and mark results on his calendar would later help me understand the process of financial savings for significant life events.

Arrival day! We traveled together by public transportation to the Philadelphia International Airport and waited for his beloved 6 p.m. flight. He paced the airport floors nervously when the flight was delayed in London, England, and then in New York City. Long past midnight, the plane arrived. As passengers departed, he painstakingly examined each passenger, finally finding the love of his life, the last to depart from the plane. He ran up to her and hugged her. While taking her hand, he prayed to thank the Lord for bringing her safely to him. Their touching of bodies, hands, and hearts became a powerful personal testimony of that great, big, wonderful God.

The man's testimony from the Republic of Zimbabwe taught me a powerful lesson about God, who is all-powerful and all-mighty. No one can perform the works He does. Only God could have given the man from Zimbabwe the strength to wait for his love. Strength to secure financial resources through personal sacrifices. Strength to study full-time and minister to others as he waits impatiently. Strength finally married his love, raised children, completed his education, and later succeeded in his chosen field. He would leave this world dying too early, but I picture him in heaven, praising the God he serves. The man from Zimbabwe is a testament to putting God first. I would be foolish not to trust him in everything, including my finances.

Frames of Reference, including both negative and positive life events, are significant and testify to a God who knows what He is doing, emphasizing the importance of trusting Him for financial peace and life. We now move to Part Two. Here is where one will see the practical resources that made up the Hicks Family's economic plan.

PART TWO: PRACTICAL

1 Timothy 5:8, "Anyone who does not provide for their relatives, and especially for their household, has denied the faith and is worse than an unbeliever." - New International Version

Figure #4

Template of the Hicks' First Family Budget 1989-90

SPENDING			INCOME		
Items	Monthly	Yearly	Item	Monthly	Yearly
NECESSITIES			**PAYROLL**		
Childcare			Spouse One		
Utilities *			Spouse Two		
Groceries					
Church Offerings			**OTHER INCOME**		
Credit Cards **			Gifts from Others		
Life Insurance			Tax Return ***		
Auto Insurance			Ministry Gift		
Auto Fuel					
Household Needs					
			SAVINGS		
			Items		
			New Home		
			Family Vacations		
ENTERTAINMENT			Family Savings		
Vacations/Day Trips			Home Maintenance Repairs		
Cable			Home Maintenance Repairs		
			Auto Maintenance Repairs		
PERSONAL			Emergencies		
Spouse One					
Spouse Two					

* Electric, Gas, Heating Oil, and Telephone   ** Paid off in two years
*** Not necessarily given or paid during the year

Chapter Five:
The Structure Budget:

Luke 14 28-30, "*Suppose you want to build a tower. You would first sit down and figure out what it costs. Then you would see if you have enough money to finish it. Otherwise, if you lay a foundation and can't finish the building, everyone who watches will make fun of you. They'll say, 'This person started to build but couldn't finish the job.'" - God Word Translation.*

SO EASY THAT A CAVEMAN CAN DO IT!

Part One of this book is a testimonial to how my family achieved financial peace. Reviewing the chapters, Chapter One provided the reason for the Hicks Family to attain financial peace through the adoption of a male child. Chapter Two explains the structures sustaining financial peace in developing a firm plan. Chapter Three describes the necessity of a financial peace on a firm financial foundation. Chapter Four introduces a frame of reference through positive and negative experiences, from which the roots of the Hicks Family's financial peace grow. In Part Two, I will give the practical resources needed when developing a budget. Chapter Five will start by understanding the structure of the Hicks Family budget.

As stated in Part One, Chapter Three, a budget is a *picture*—a pictographic portrait showing income and spending. To further explain, a budget is a written plan that oversees and controls one's financial resources. It must not be viewed as a negative tool. Though it can bring light to damaging financial practices, a budget can help identify and monitor them, giving insight into areas needing correction, improvement, or maintenance. In an unstable national and global economy driven by greed, war, and unstructured attitudes, it is crucial to take one's finances seriously. Not taking finances seriously will cause uncontrollable debt, poor credit scores, emotional distress, and family breakups.

Confronted with the enormous responsibility of raising a son, it was logical for me to investigate templates of successful budgets. Quickly, I discovered obstacles. Though my wife Diane and I worked with church budgets, I was unprepared for the different types, forms, and designs of budgets, all developed to meet various needs. There were templates of budgets addressing payroll concerns, budgets for marketing, budgets for hospital use, budgets for future projects, and budgets for events (sporting, musical, educational, etc.). Templates that had line graphs with color codes and geometric shapes. Although many budget templates were available, I couldn't use them because my family's needs weren't significant enough to support these types of budgets. I don't remember that "HA-HA" moment; however, I knew the budget required must be easy to understand and serviceable. It is best described in a television commercial aired twenty-three years later.

In 2012, the Partner Marketing Group developed a commercial for an insurance company with the catchy phrase, "**So Easy a Caveman Can Do it.**"[40] The ad campaign with the words became very successful because it met the following criteria for good marketing, keeping the target audience looking for more... It had humor; people were more likely to recall humorous ideas. They played continuously and consistently on multiple media platforms. The message was "simple" for those who struggle to understand life insurance's complexity. Though the saying was established after the family budget was developed, it answered the question of what constituted a first serviceable budget. The budget that would meet my family's needs must be so simple that Diane and I, without financial expertise, could understand and use it. The chart at the beginning of this chapter, *Figure #4,* is the template the Hicks Family found serviceable from 1989 to 1990.

The budget template developed was simple and easy because it was tailored to the family's needs. It was also personal, for it was saturated with the family's personality and preferences. When one saw the budget, it was as if one held it up to a mirror; one would see the Hicks Family. It mirrored the family preferences, which included the family's values, through items of importance.

---

[40] GEICO Insurance

The family's hopes and dreams, painted on paper, summarize the family's present and future needs and desires. Structured under the three categories **"Spending, Income, and Savings."** It did not make sense to have a complicated budget requiring many financial types. It was important that Diane and I could quickly understand, communicate, and follow. Later, as the family secured their first home, they considered several factors, including Benjamin's growth, family health challenges, planning for retirement, fluctuations in income, and purchasing a second home, when formatting future budgets to meet these and other challenges. To better understand these three categories, let's view each separately.

THE THREE CATEGORIES!

Spending!

A budget is valuable because it provides insight into where the money is spent. One would think I should have started by showing how money is received. I began with spending because it shows the **"what and the why."** The **what** explains the family spending habits. Its purpose is to identify and evaluate the habits that influence the composition of a budget. As the budget is developed, these essential spending habits become line items. The **why** asks about the necessity of spending. Spending can be emotionally motivated by desires, wants, and things seen and felt. It can be witnessed in the forms of luxury spending, spurge spending, mental health spending, overspending, crisis spending, and non-budget spending. Answering the why question provides insight into correcting undesirable expenditures.

For some, keeping track of spending is hard work. It was not for us. It was effortless to record expenditures by asking for receipts. Once receipts were received, they were immediately recorded under their respective line item. This proved the easiest to perform because we were serious and dedicated to the process. However, speaking with others, I understood that some found this difficult. Some said it took more time and a more significant effort to remember to keep records of all expenditures with receipts. By keeping records, some family members did not want others to discover receipts for their self-centered spending habits. It is imperative to be honest and accurate, not allowing personal biases and embarrassment to stop the budget process. For the Hicks family, requesting and recording receipts is vital to monitoring responsible spending. After reviewing my family's spending habits, I found it logical to begin organizing the spending portion by looking at it closely.

The category of Spending was broken down into three divisions. The first under-spending is…

NECESSITIES		
Childcare		
Utilities *		
Groceries		
Church Offerings		
Credit Cards **		
Life Insurance		
Auto Insurance		
Auto Fuel		
Household Needs		

Necessities. (*Figure #5*)

It represented the largest spending line item that the family could not live without. These items are essential to the health and welfare of the family. Figure #5 lists the necessary items the Hicks Family needed to sustain a simple existence. As explained in Part One, Chapter One, items involving the home were one of the most significant necessities. I learned of its importance from a question asked by a student in a social studies class at Philadelphia College of Bible in the Spring of 1973.[41] The student asks, *"Why will members of one culture spend money on a new car and live in a house in disrepair?"* After a meaningful and engaging discussion, the class concluded that cultural

---

[41] Now known as Carin University

values were the core. Cultural values can be seen in the Nomadic tribes of Africa, which place a higher value on serviceable animals transporting humans and their prized possessions. A non-serviceable animal was worthless. These nomadic tribes were always on the move. Permanent structures were not needed. They would construct temporary shelters from materials brought or found along the journey. Though respectful towards cultures that pay greater attention to the necessity and preservation of all modes of transportation, the Hicks Family felt that the home and all that connected to it were more critical.

All resources should point to those necessary items connected to the upkeep and maintenance of the home. As seen above, a listing of the required subdivision items the Hicks Family needed to survive. Although some listed items may not be considered home items at first glance (Church Offerings, Child Care, Groceries, Auto, Insurance, Credit Cards). They became critical in providing my wife, Diane, and me the means to maintain the home. It is ridiculous for my family to live without understanding the indispensable need to keep a roof over our heads. Necessities not only track but remind the family that money must be used, and I repeat, must be used, every month without fail, to uphold such a valuable landmark.

The second spending division is **entertainment** (*Figure #6*), **which includes** enjoyable activities for personal satisfaction.

Item	Monthly	Yearly
ENTERTAINMENT		
Vacations/Day Trips		
Cable		

Though small, they prove to be needed as the family journeys through life. The emotional strain of life became overwhelming, and spending money on entertainment reduced the pressure. If there was guilt, it was lifted, knowing that money was set aside for enjoyment. There was no luxury spending. Day trips were spent driving to local beaches or historical locations that offered economically friendly activities. Then there were the one-week vacations, as previously stated, usually in Virginia Beach. We stayed in apartment-type residences, which included a kitchen. This replaced the cost of eating at restaurants, using the savings to further the family's entertainment needs. Being close to outdoor activities, including movie theaters and sporting events, was necessary. These allowed the family to play together and have fun. As in the saying, "All work and no play makes

Johnny a dull boy."[42] Cable television allowed the family to stay indoors and enjoy each other's company by watching family-friendly movies and television shows. The last responsible spending division is **Personal**.

Personal (*Figure #7*)

Item	Monthly	Yearly
PERSONAL		
Spouse One		
Spouse Two		

Here is where the saying, "Pay yourself first," was used, and Diane and I took full advantage. Diane and I opened personal checking, credit cards, and savings accounts. We both wanted to be financially independent, allowing us to spend money without compromising the family's needs. In addition, Diane and I would not have to explain personal spending. However, for budgeting purposes, spending without the name of the items purchased was counted against the family budget as line items under our names. For Diane, having control over her money helped her in the long run, giving her the experience of understanding money management. Chapter Six of this book will reveal more information about this account.

---

[42] All work and no play makes Jack a dull boy - Wikipedia

Income!

A budget would be dead on arrival without an income source. Income to a budget is like the steering wheel of a car. One can steer the budget in a precise direction for a purpose. Without revenue, there would be no spending, no budget, and, for the Hicks Family, no ability to obtain a house. The original purpose for starting a budget was to find a home to care for our son. My wife and I did not have wealthy relatives to shower us with money or income we could immediately spend. Some Christian friends said I took God out of the equation by having an income section in the budget. God, who is all-powerful and mighty, can produce more money than needed at the snap of his fingers. Though true, this idea has been misrepresented by many of my brothers and sisters in Christ. They promote the belief that God does not desire His children to be poor, but rather to be rich through practicing correct thinking and financially donating to the church.[43] Though I disagree with this belief, I refuse to dismiss God from the equation. God has not failed to provide resources for my family's needs. God can and will

---

[43] Prosperity gospel | Definition, Origins, History, Theology, Criticism, & Facts | Britannica

supply all things for his children. As I continue to repeat, God's means and purposes are for his glory and his children's benefit.

"**Payroll**," the first income subdivision, was the line item where Diane and I recorded paychecks.

"**Payroll** (*Figure #8*)

Item	Monthly	Yearly
PAYROLL		
Spouse One		
Spouse Two		

We recorded our monthly and yearly income, which gave us an idea of the money we could spend each month and year. The monthly and annual amounts sometimes change because of raises, bonuses, unemployment, and paycheck delays. This was more helpful than obstructive because it allowed for careful spending. Payroll is not the family's only income source; they also receive money from a second income source.

"**Other Income.**" (*Figure #9)*

Items	Monthly	Yearly
OTHER INCOME		
Gifts from Others		
Tax Return***		
Ministry Gifts		

This second income subdivision, though received sporadically, helped "fill in the gap" when extra revenue was needed. These incomes came from preaching/ministry opportunities, gifts from friends, found monies, and sometimes from federal and state tax returns.

All income received was made possible by the grace of God. Could God bless the Hicks Family without gainful employment, tax returns, or gifts? Yes. God can and does bless using supernatural means. I have heard stories of God securing a job for a needy family and supplying money to pay off a debt at the "ninth hour," and many other miraculous stories. My family also experienced this. I opened a letter without a return address three months into the budget. Inside, I found one hundred and fifty dollars. The unexpected gift was used to pay an unexpected bill. It became a testimony that God continues to look after us. To this day, I have not found the person who gave the family such a wonderful gift. I can only credit God. Again, I repeat it: God does all for his glory and his children's benefit. The Savings category was developed to complete the budget, providing additional resources to make our dreams come true.

Savings!

Items	Monthly	Yearly
New Home		
Family Vacation		
Family Savings		
Home Maintenance/Repairs		
Auto Maintenance/Repairs		
Emergencies		
Federal Tax Payment ***		

Savings (*Figure #10*)

Savings is a category where money is set aside for future events. Benjamin Franklin coined the phrase, "A penny saved is two pence clear." Today, the wording changes from "two pence clear to the penny earned," but the meaning does not change." When one puts money aside and does not spend, it becomes income for later use. I mention my father, who held on to a dollar until it hollered. Though a selfish act, it is an act that pays enormous dividends. We saw how true the saying was when the family took Mr. Herb Denenberg's advice. Saving for a home and enjoying life were not the only purposes. The family needed to have a stash of money available for unexpected needs. Let's not forget the repairs and maintenance mentioned in Part One of this book, nor the unplanned emergencies that always steal the joys of living. Saving is an approach one takes if one wants independence from creditors and financial peace of mind. I found the following thoughts helpful as I pursued making savings work for me...

- "Never say you don't have the money to save!" You have money to save if you receive a paycheck, gifts, government assistance, from begging, from friends and family, or retirement holdings.
- "It is never too early or too late to save!" It makes financial sense to start saving earlier in life. However, starting today is better, as it delays the chance of a missed opportunity tomorrow.
- "Amount one puts away does not matter!" Save whatever amount you feel comfortable with. It is better to save something than nothing.
- "Be consistent!" Many people get in trouble because they start saving but later stop. After consistently banking one bi-weekly paycheck for eighteen months, I built savings of over ten thousand dollars. The more one puts away, the more one earns.

- "Place money in the hands of friends or relatives" when tempted to spend on unnecessary items. My late brother Charles, fearing he wouldn't have enough money to pay his bills, asked relatives to hold onto cash until his bills were due.

- "Limit the use of cash apps!" My grandnephew became upset when he asked his grandmother for money from his checking account. He learned he had spent over two hundred dollars ordering food from a fast food app.

- "Limit the use of credit cards!" Credit cards are helpful if used wisely. Always pay the monthly balance due, guarding against paying interest fees and accumulating large credit card balances.

CRUNCHING THE BUDGET NUMBERS!

Can I add a new pet to the household, pay for the summer vacation plans, or keep cable television? When analyzing the numbers that motivated me to maintain a workable family budget, I faced these questions yearly. Financial experts call this "crunching the numbers. Crunching budget numbers is an incredibly involved fiscal activity. It consists of calculating the budget cost by summing the expenses under line items and determining the income availability to cover it. Spending under some line items is straightforward, for their cost are stable. Examples include insurance payments, mortgage or rental payments, childcare, and church offerings. Others can be more difficult because they fluctuate throughout the year, with some changes driven by family use, such as utility/fuel consumption, and groceries. The key is to organize their purpose and importance to the family's survival.

Crushing the numbers, the lesson learned, and the ongoing reality is that family survival is paramount. Because of the need for family survival, the family and I had to balance our "Wants and Needs." The **wants** are things desired; the **needs** are essentials. If mishandled, I found that wants and needs can create an unstable family dichotomy. For example, the family wanted to keep the cable television purchased before the initial budget. Crushing the numbers found that continuing to pay for cable television (a want) would not fit. Nevertheless, we decided to keep it in the budget. However, at the end of the budget's first year, it became clear that the family could no longer afford it, as it took money away from other essential items. With that, cable was taken out of the following year's budget. It returned thirty years after the family purchased a condominium, a benefit found in the HOA fees.[44]

Success can be achieved. A few of the suggestions were mentioned in the narrative of this book, and I remembered other tips as I formulated my thoughts. All of this helped me crush the budget numbers and continue today successfully. Let me summarize the steps I learned…

The **first step** in developing the numbers for a budget is to know the income for the year. This is found in knowing the amount of income from employment or any other income stream (*Figures #8 & #9).* Though income numbers are in flux because family members receive bonuses, raises, layoffs, salary reductions, or other causes, adjustments can be made as they occur. Add up all the income numbers, then divide by twelve (months in a year) to find the monthly income available. The **second step** is deciding what can or cannot be paid. Once one gets a firm idea of expected income numbers, start listing, as seen in spending under "Necessities" or *needs.* They represent the most important areas of spending. The numbers can be found by knowing monthly payment amounts through word

---

[44] HOA (Home Owners Association). They are individuals elected by the residents of a housing complex, setting the rules and fees that maintain the complex.

of mouth, written bills, or notices. After satisfying "Necessities," distribute monies for Entertainment and Personal. They can be looked at as *wants*. Remember to put money away in Savings. Savings will become income to cover unplanned spending or to fulfill special needs or desires. **Lastly**, review the budget monthly. As stated in this book, it will allow you to track income and spending. You do not want to be placed in a situation where being unprepared causes financial harm. At the end of this chapter, I put the final numbers of my 1989-90 family budget.

In conclusion, a budget is an essential resource for families to help them understand money as it is spent and received. Without a sound budget, one's life will travel like a ship without a rudder or sails. Nothing guides a family to a peaceful financial harbor but a budget. The next chapter will help you start by looking at the physical and financial platforms supporting the budget.

Figure #11

HICKS FAMILY FINAL BUDGET FOR 1989-90

(Amounts Approximated)

SPENDING $14,436.00			INCOME $29,650.70		
Items	Monthly	Yearly	Item	Monthly	Yearly
NECESSITIES	$736.00	$9,156.00	PAYROLL	$2,435.88	$29,230.70
Childcare	$240.00	$2,88.00	Spouse One	$1,297.86	$15,574.30
Utilities *	$95.00	$1,140.00	Spouse Two	$1,138.02	$13,656.30
Groceries	$230.00	$2,760.00			
Church Offerings	$25.00	$300.00	OTHER INCOME	$35.00	$420.00
Credit Cards **	$45.00	$540.00	Gifts from Others	$10.00	$120.00
Life Insurance	$38.00	$456.00	Tax Return ***	Unknown	
Auto Insurance	$25.00	$300.00	Ministry Gift	$25.00	$300.00
Auto Fuel	$25.00	$540.00			
Household Needs	25.00	$300.00			
			SAVINGS	$795.00	$9,720.00
			Items	Monthly	Yearly
			New Home	$675.00	8,100.00
			Family Vacations	$25.00	$300.00
ENTERTAINMENT	$50.00	$780.00	Family Savings	$25.00	$300.00
Vacations/Day Trips	$30.00	$540.00	Home Maintenance Repairs	$25.00	$300.00
Cable	$20.00	$240.00	Auto Maintenance Repairs	$30.00	$540.00
			Emergencies	$15.00	$180.00
PERSONAL	$310.00	$3720.00	Federal Income Tax ***	Unknown	
Spouse One	$160.00	$1,920.00			
Spouse Two	$150.00	$1,800.00			

Chapter Six:

FINANCIAL PLATFORM TYPES:

Romans 12:6, *Having gifts that differ according to the grace given to us, let us use them:* -English Standard Version.

A PHYSICAL FINANCIAL PLATFORM

The budget you are reading is an example of my LORD giving my wife and me the minds to examine the needs and wants of the family, using our limited income to develop a format for survival and financial peace amidst a growing family and the economic pressures it faces. It is relevant to my family's past, present, and future use. I will always thank the Lord for his wisdom. This same wisdom showed us that the budget was inoperable unless backed up by a physical presence. It needed a physical, financial platform.

A platform is a raised, flat physical structure used to explain political policies or principles, types of software in computer systems, and service-oriented websites or applications.[45] A more identifiable platform is found in public transportation stations. Here, people wait to board or debark as they go to and from their destinations. Along platforms, one will discover notices used to give directions to modes of transportation, street-level communication, and public information areas. Securing users' safety and well-

---

[45] platforms examples - Search (bing.com) February 26, 2024

being is nearly impossible without a robust, user-friendly, and secure platform.

Some may say there is no difference between a financial platform and a financial structure. For the Hicks financial plan, there is. In Chapter Two of this book, I explain what holds the family's financial structure, which is **"a budget plan."** In this chapter, the financial platform supports the actual physical budget, providing easy accessibility for protected and disbursed funds, a manager for assistance, and modern equipment for budget tracking. Without it, the final budget, though reasonable on paper, is just that, reasonable. Let's examine the physical platforms needed to achieve financial peace for my family.

Account Types!

Securing financial accounts is a crucial aspect of maintaining a secure financial platform. These accounts facilitate ensuring financial peace. They are where financial resources are held in commercial banks and tracked monthly. I'd like to introduce three beneficial account types.

- **First, "Primary Account Type."** Also called *"Family Accounts,"* they comprised checking, savings, and vacation accounts. Money is used to pay all family bills and expenses. This consists of all items found in the spending category under necessary budget items. **The checking account,** which *I call the bill payer*, should contain what one must spend each month. I found it comforting to have at least five hundred dollars more in the account to pay all monthly obligations and minimize bank maintenance fees. In 1989, I paid bills to vendors with paper checks. With the high cost of paper checks and the advent of free bank checks, payments are now delivered to vendors electronically. **The savings account** is essential to sound money management. Setting aside money monthly builds up a reserve for existing family projects. These reserves can be transferred into the checking account when additional funds are needed. Also called the *"rainy day account,"* it is money set aside for future desires. To pay for expected and unexpected expenses. [46] **The Vacation Account,** or

---

[46] Just in case situations. Situations that were either unexpected or unplanned.

"relaxation account," saves money for yearly vacations and family activities. It was satisfying to have a separate account for the fun things in life, separate from checking and savings. Lastly, **Credit Card Account**. This account is used when paying with a credit card is more manageable. Whatever the balance at the end of the month must be paid in full. For each family account, the family was obligated to obtain permission from one another whenever spending over five hundred dollars. If consent is not given, the money is not spent.

- **Second, "Private Individual Account Types."** As previously discussed, my wife, Diane, and I maintain separate financial accounts from the family. These accounts allow us to manage our own money. In addition, it will enable us to spend money without the guilt of using funds intended for the family. We don't need to ask each other for permission to spend personal money, regardless of the amount. However, by agreement, the money from the accounts is included in the family budget. This allows both to maintain financial accountability and give aid whenever one has difficulty with their accounts. For my wife, Diane, it provides knowledge that she may need to manage and maintain the family finances if I am unable to do so.

- **Third, "Retirement Accounts Types."** Fifteen years into the budget, as responsibilities grew and we became aware of our mortality, my wife Diane and I understood that the family needed to save for retirement. The accounts contained money to be used as income when the needs arrived. It was important not to withdraw from these accounts until necessary, either due to government restrictions or other circumstances.[47] Although we should have started when the initial budget was developed, it was beneficial that we recognized the need and opened retirement accounts "sooner rather than later."

A Manager that Assists: The Financial Advisor

Chapter Two states that using a financial advisor as a counselor is beneficial. As an economic platform, it can

---

[47] Some IRA Retirement Accounts require withdrawals that are age-related. Presently, it is 71 years old.

be both beneficial and costly. The Bureau of Labor Statistics (BLS), in its 2023 report, states that the average hourly rate for an accountant or *financial advisor* is thirty-seven dollars an hour. This fee depends on the accountant's experience and one's personal/business needs.[48] However, don't let the cost interfere with helping develop a sound financial strategy. We already discussed the downfall of not having a strategy, which costs money and compromises the family's security. Look for ways to lower the price to be less taxing on the budget plan. Here are a few ways... Place the cost of an advisor into the family budget. Decrease spending in one or more expense line items. Seek to increase income through part-time employment or other income-generating opportunities. Investing in an excellent financial advisor will be in your best interest. When I began, I was intimidated and frustrated trying to maneuver through the many types of accounts, especially retirement accounts. My financial advisor taught me that retirement accounts are investment accounts. They took various forms: real estate, individual retirement, stocks, bonds, insurance policies, and annuities. I can confidently say that securing a sound financial advisor helps relieve the stress. My financial advisors steered the family to the retirement

---

[48] How Much Does An Accountant Cost In 2023? – Forbes Advisor

accounts that offered the best value. For fifteen years, the family has enjoyed advice from four financial advisors. In the last five years, the family has enjoyed the advice and the relationship developed with our present advisor. The guidance has been "spot on" and has created a bond of mutual trust and respect, making me feel comfortable knowing the advisor has my family's financial interest in mind.

At the same time, the family has appreciated the legal advice of an attorney. However, they can be more expensive than financial advisors. The initial consultation may be free, but securing their services can cost hundreds of dollars an hour. I hired different attorneys to provide my family with legal information to make timely decisions regarding real estate purchases, financial concerns, and estate issues. Relationships have been more professional than personal. The last chapter will provide a detailed description of one attorney's work addressing the family's legal needs.

Modern Equipment to Track the Budget: Computer Software

As with financial advisors and attorneys, a computer and its accompanying financial software can be expensive. To help develop the initial budget, the Hicks family used an electric typewriter. It helped create a simple spreadsheet that was easy to read and to input financial data. However, the data could not talk back to us. It was not just enough to see the information. It needed to inform us about the status of the money, comparing it with the previous month's spending, and outline the means for future spending and savings. The family decided to spend money to purchase a computer. We were fortunate to have a ready-made financial program installed with a Microsoft program. The program, "Money." Although the program has discontinued answering online questions, we continue to use it. Though other financial software programs exist, I have found Money user-friendly and free for over thirty years. When the time comes, I will consider another financial software.

What should a financial computer program do? As stated, it should be interactive or "talk back." **First,** one should be able to open and see all financial records and holdings immediately. The Money program is divided into categories. The category **Accounts** shows where the Hicks Family holds its funds. They are held in financial institutions, including all family and personal accounts (checking and savings), as well as online accounts, or are secured in the family's safe. The Credit Cards category shows the family's credit cards and balances (if any) they contain. The category **Retirement** offers retirement accounts that my financial advisor secures. At the time of writing, all retirement accounts are under one financial institution, which controls all the family's accounts. In the past, retirement accounts were spread out among several financial retirement institutions. The category **Others** shows items that are not accounts or retirement. They include market values of the family home, automobile, cemetery plot, and any assets we oversee. Secondly, one should be able to generate daily, weekly, monthly, and yearly reports of income and spending. This is where our financial state spoke loudly. These reports provided a snapshot of the family's financial holdings, revealing their financial health or instability. The reports can be printed and distributed to family members to provide accountability and directions as the family moves forward.

A good computer financial software program can help those needing assistance in developing a budget. The Money software program allows one to create a budget with step-by-step instructions based on the financial information input.

Finding an excellent financial computer software program is significant. Though I found software meeting the family's needs, I do not want to dismiss the many other software programs in the market. Time should be spent developing a financial strategy before securing a computer software program. Once it is found, continue its use until the program becomes obsolete or unable to meet the need. Though the next is the final chapter of this book, it is not the last chapter of the Hicks Family's financial story.

CHAPTER SEVEN

"THE SECOND VISION"

"What will happen to our hard-earned financial resources after death?"

Habakkuk 2:3, *For still the vision awaits its appointed time; it hastens to the end— it will not lie. If it seems slow, wait for it; it will surely come; it will not delay.* - English Standard Version

The story continues with both old and new challenges. The old is found in life's daily, monthly, and yearly financial obligations. The necessities of life (i.e., food, clothing, taxes, fees, etc.) continue without an end. And, of course, balancing these necessities with the money available in bank and retirement accounts. As Diane and I enter the twilight of life, new challenges unfold. We question if balancing daily, monthly, and yearly obligations with available funds would be our final epitaph. Death is the lot for all people. No one knows where or when they will breathe their last breath. This led to a question that required an answer. That question... *__What will happen to our hard-earned financial resources after death?__* The question caused feelings of unrest as we continued our financial journey. Again, we seek peace. As the first vision of financial peace was given through the words of Herb Denenberg, a second vision was needed from the Lord to identify how our remaining funds would be distributed and who would benefit. This would be our final peace.

As Diane and I pondered the question, two things came into view. First, the reality of natural human behavior regarding wealth is left to the beneficiaries. This I call the **"Agreement."** Second, the **"Answer,"** which is the second vision of the Lord, allows us to respond positively, resolving the question. Follow me as I share how these two words brought another form of financial peace.

"What will happen to our hard-earned financial resources after death?"

The Agreement: You Can't Take It with You! [49]

Of course, you cannot take your wealth (great or small) to either heaven or hell. Instead, for many families, wealth is passed down from generation to generation. Various families did not start with wealth. Their founders made their wealth in several ways. Many found wealth working in their communities as peddlers, tailors, or merchants. Some borrowed from family and friends, creating inventions that made wealth. Others achieve success through shrewd or shady business dealings, or by being at the right place at the right time. As the founders grew older and realized they could not "take it with them," they passed the wealth to family members, freeing them from the trials and tribulations and the struggles to survive. In some families, the passing down of wealth has led to a

---

[49] Term expressing that physical possessions cannot follow a person to death.

"holier than thou" attitude among family members. [50] Though many did not intend to, others like to show off their wealth in the homes they live in, the vehicles they drive, and the fashions they own. In addition, they had contempt for those not in their financial social circles.

Diane and I drew up a will years after we purchased our first home. It was not just for financial security for surviving family members; we wanted to be good stewards of our money in death as we were in life, and the will outlined our wishes in the event of our deaths. Our only son became the executive and the only beneficiary. It is not unusual for surviving adult children to be executives and beneficiaries of their parents. If children are involved, they are responsible for working together to ensure their parents' estate is settled agreeably. This was true when my father, the surviving parent, left farming property given to him from his father to me and my four siblings. My older sister and I handled contacts with realtors, potential buyers, and county officials. We reported to the other two siblings (the younger brother had died) on the progress or lack thereof. My sisters agreed on a selling price and were willing to adjust it if the eventual purchaser presented a different

---

[50] Thinking one is greater or better in words or deeds than another.

offer. This is not true in many families. A family with several adult children who are beneficiaries can cause significant infighting when executing a family estate. Even when the surviving child is the only beneficiary, battles can develop between the one beneficiary and with relatives from both sides of the family lines and friends who believe they deserve a "piece of the pie.[51]" This is why I suggest that all parents outline the disposition of their financial affairs in a will. It is the personal satisfaction of knowing, though one cannot take it with them. You can determine who can benefit.

After moving to another state and family-related issues, we felt our will needed to be reviewed. So, Diane and I sought out the help of an estate attorney. The attorney reviewed our will and asked about the family's financial holdings. We were pleased that he saw no immediate changes needed moving forward. This should have satisfied the question while sealing the Hicks family's epilogue, but it did not. Instead, the second vision satisfied the question. Satisfaction comes from knowing that our hard-earned financial resources would serve as an epilogue,

---

[51] A word used in business when the business starts making money for the owner, others want to benefit.

bringing glory and honor to our Lord. That second vision came from an unexpected source: my younger sister.

What will happen to our hard-earned financial resources after death?"

The Answer: The Second Vision!

As stated, it was my younger sister whom the Lord provided to my wife Diane and me that second vision. It began with my sister and me discussing the money Diane and I had accumulated over the years. Our financial holdings, though comfortable, were not like those of the rich and famous. We used money from our checking account to meet the many monthly necessities of life. Money in our savings and retirement accounts (not truckloads of cash) was available to meet emergencies and promote confidence. It was less significant than that of financial giants like Jeff Bezos and Elon Musk. However, if there were no substantial critical financial expenses, it would be enough for the family to pay for essentials and necessities for the rest of our lives. Then my sister asked, *"Why do you need that much money?"* I saw puzzlement in her expression because I didn't immediately offer a response. As you have experienced in this book, my family's journey to financial peace was, in part, due to sacrificial, unwarranted, and careful savings. I would eventually share that with her, hopefully ending the conversation. Not receiving the answers she was looking for, she reframed the question and asked, *"What will happen to your hard-earned financial resources after death?"* Then I began to understand it. Her question was not about the family's past needs; she asked about the family's present and future needs. My response to her question birthed the second vision,

As the first vision, the second vision immediately brought answers to mind, proving to be the direction I need to follow if Diane and I have a definitive epilogue. Since the process of distributing the family's financial resources was in place within the original will, we were ahead of the game. Although the estate attorney found no fault, Diane and I believed it was necessary to be more transparent for all parties involved. We are now prepared to give clear instructions for distributing our financial resources amongst families and non-profits. Therefore, Diane and I will submit an addendum to the will for processing by the estate attorney. This is the crust of the second vision. At the time of writing, the family has not finalized the addendum; however, the following summarizes the three main points.

- **Family:** Seventy-five percent of the remaining retirement or money remaining in bank accounts will be set aside for surviving children, grandchildren, nieces, nephews, or siblings. The distribution of the funds will be handled by the surviving spouse or child of the oldest surviving relative. The remaining twenty-five percent will be set aside for a non-profit organization.
- **Non-profits:** are non-profit religious or non-religious organizations providing services to people experiencing poverty or those in need.
- **Diane and Otis:** Insurance money will be used for funeral arrangements. All other money will be distributed at the discretion of the surviving spouse, our surviving son, or our oldest surviving relative. Portions of cash from savings and checking accounts, at our discretion, will be used for us to enjoy as health allows. We refuse to live defeated lives. We will plan vacations and make our home comfortable with upgrades and repairs. In addition,

we will purchase our final automobile and treat ourselves daily.

Is spending on ourselves a selfish desire? I let you be the judge. All I know is that God gave my wife and me the financial means to care for our son for forty years and counting, for business and personal needs, and to others in need. Why not for ourselves as we face death? We can only thank God for providing us with what we needed to meet our many needs in times of plenty and scarcity. Our epilogue is now complete. We now know *"What will happen to our hard-earned financial resources?"*

Do You?

Conclusion

Proverbs 16:9, *"Man can make plans, but the Lord establishes the steps."*

I thank you for your willingness to read the testimony of the Hicks Family in their quest to achieve financial peace in an unstable world. In addition, thank you for your patience as I explained this quest, which took many turns and detours. You have read the testimony on how a financial plan was established to aid in the development of a male child, my wife Diane and I adopted, because his birth mother did not have the means to care for him. It did not just benefit this man-child; it helped Diane and me grow closer to God by trusting Him in all things. We experienced the faithfulness of our Lord despite my many acts of disobedience and unfaithfulness, which could have destroyed the little I had. And how the Lord gave the family two visions of financial peace through His mercy and grace in the person of Herb Denenberg and my younger sister. Lastly, we experienced the challenges and trials along the journey. I pray that reading gave you concepts you will consider in the coming days, weeks, and even years to come.

The conclusion I give is written in the pages of this book. It is a conclusion built on my advice if you desire financial peace, not prosperity, amidst your financial storms. To summarize, my advice, as found in the pages of this book, is to plan your finances well by building a workable budget and caring for the present needs while planning for future needs. Set aside money for emergencies, but don't forget the affordable, entertaining things in life. As you age, consider using retirement savings for relaxing activities you might not have thought of due to concerns about the family's immediate needs. Don't stop trusting in the Lord. Use the mind God gave you, but with it, rely on the power of God to provide you with the best insight and direction. As Proverbs 16:9 states, *"Man can make plans, but the Lord establishes the steps."*

All praises to God!
Amen!

Written by
Otis Benjamin Hicks Jr. © 2025

_____